PURIFICATION

CLEANSING OF A
CONTAMINATED SOUL

John Dervishian

authorHOUSE®

AuthorHouse™
1663 Liberty Drive
Bloomington, IN 47403
www.authorhouse.com
Phone: 1-800-839-8640

First published by AuthorHouse   5/5/2009

ISBN: 978-1-4389-7626-6 (sc)

Printed in the United States of America
Bloomington, Indiana

This book is printed on acid-free paper.

To my wife and beautiful daughters

ACKNOWLEDGEMENTS

Alvin Riley

Selvin Chambers

Albert U Turner

Dianne Chalifour

CONTENTS

INTRODUCTION

The words within this book do not discriminate. There have been many experiences that have brought me to the point of being able to transcribe feelings onto paper, in a subtle but passionate way. In a world seen through the eyes of beauty and pain, these words will transcend the traditional world of poetry.

The first time I picked up a pen I was "high" and was at a loss in life. I felt distant from family and had lost friends along the way. I used drugs and alcohol as a way to overcome pain and adapt to life. I "socially" used drugs/alcohol but I know it was all to secrete my emotions. The day I looked up and saw what I had written on paper was the day that set me free, a day that allowed me to speak. That was twenty years ago. Twenty years of discovering life, and learning from each new experience. My thoughts, expressions and words collected on paper: words that help me convey my feelings. I discovered a new way to overcome pain and express myself. I continue to strive and reach new goals for the future.

UNSURE

First was the seed that needed to be soiled with love
Then the roots that extend out with open arms
Now grown up with love to give
One day asks, what is love?

Love is filled equally with happiness and pain

A NEW DRUG

Is it the sun that makes you smile?
Is it the rain that makes you sad?
Take a little taste of the drops
Everyone does it
Don't be a fool
Feel from it, learn from it
See what it's like when
the sun and rain mix
It's an unforgettable high
that lasts forever.

WITHOUT PEACE

I am not bonded with family
but reunited with life
My experiences cast pictures
of being taught
I regained strength and intelligence
by living
The darkness is my surrounding
A good high taught me to speak
and express
Motivation and thought
will lead me to inner freedom.

SILENCE....

She dances in the blaze of fire
With each bright step
bringing me higher
Mesmerizing me with each
glowing stare
Refusing me the soft touch
of her hair
I sit and watch her spin
round and round
While she lifts my soul
above the ground
Listening as she speaks
like the singing of angels
she has my mind

confused and tangled
I reach to touch her smooth skin
and knowing this feeling
she makes me happy within
She knows that I adore
her beautiful kind
Even without speaking
she can read my mind.

VETERAN

We met during a war
A fight within herself
Confused, lonely
I took the advantage
of becoming her ally
A soldier in the night
I captured her mind and soul
We became lovers

Ecstasy is what won the war
Hatred is what lost it.

VAGABOND

Waiting for friends
A man walks up, staggering and drunk
holding a sandwich
He says he won $5,000.00
on ten scratch tickets
He gave $3500.00 to his mother
and spent the rest on his habit
He shakes my hand, then goes
on his way
Before his departure he said
"if you see my mother, tell her
I said hi".

MISSING....

Whispers in the wind
Sound like thousands
of your voices
People in crowds
all look like you
The feeling of raindrops
are like the sweet touch
of your hands.

Touch of rain
The warm wind
Voices in the dark
What does this mean?

UNDER THE INFLUENCE

An empty bottle of Jack Daniels
A midnight run to a package store
that's closed
A heart full of rage and violence
A man, a bystander, in the way
It is a menial obstacle

Steel bars, one window
and a cot
15 years to go!!

A FREE HIGH

I am experiencing a new drug
A much more predominant high
No needles, no pipes or papers
No hallucinations, no delusions
No distortions or side effects
This high is not illegal and cannot
be weighed in ounces or grams
Just beauty touching my soul.

START NEW

Sit home quietly
Collect life in a bottle
then smash it!!

THE END

Lying on a warm swept floor
Holding on to a stopwatch
Time ticking away, waiting
for the strike of the needle
Life is catching up
Not much to do here
Tick
Tick
Stop!

REFRESHED

Wake up a new day is dawn
There is a perplexed image in life
You swept out the past,
for you were not served
Lean on the outside
Don't fall over.

DOCTRINES OF SOCIETY

Lollipop skirts and ponytails
A molester's dream
Matches and gasoline
An arson's tool
The government and their hobbies
Reason for world debt
Racism, crime and violence
Societies products
Why?

NEW VENTURE

How's life? Ok
How's death? Unknown
So what's the matter?
There's a knock on my door
Too tired to open, who is it?
Oh nice to see you
How's life? Ok
How's death? Known

(Excuses for death
Justification for life
Who the hell cares)

EXCUSES

But, need, yes, no, trust
Space, because, too much, time
Maybe, never, heard, because
I don't know

I, you. Me
Friends
Enough words used too frequently.

NO END IN SIGHT

A short ride that gets longer
People shuffling back and forth
grasping on to their sanity for security

Do you hear the children screaming?
Yearning for comfort?
Are you aware of the storm that's developing?
The thrashing of the thunder vibrates in my head
where's the sun?

I need still waters
with
A
Clear view

VERSES

It's said,
"money makes the world go round"
Well, I'm dizzy and want to get off

Should I, should we
Spontaneous would be nice!

MONOTONY...

The sun rose as usual
I showered and got dressed the same
Went on my way like I always do
Saw the same people again
Where's the thrill?

The sun set
It's dark and the lights are still
bothering my eyes
I go through this all the time
Why continue?

The sun rose and set,
So nice to see your
radiant image

Here's the thrill.

DAYDREAMING

Often dream off into a world
of my own
No one can find me there
A place where there are
no doubts and only serenity
What a place to find
No such thing as time or limits
Where all desires and dreams come true
What a place to find.

MARTYR

Sacrifice for another
for the quick pleasure
The storm is coming
Town whores walk up and down
collecting their fares
Cars passing by
An accident occurs
One person injured
Another dead
Where does his soul go mommy?
What's next?
Who's next?
Hello, is anyone there?
I'm lost, where are we?

STRANGER...

We spoke to each other once
But you did not understand
You led me into your heart
as a friend
Not by your hand

You enthuse me by your wit
Seduce me with your smile
This game has been playing
for such a long while.

REPETITIVE PAIN

The closing of the night brings
on sounds of thought
Of you and I together,
sharing each other
and being taught

I can't bear the pain
of not being near
When my one wish
is to look, touch and hear

The blood races with passion
to my mind
With the feeling of light
that I need to find.

SHALL WE DANCE?

Shall we dance to the beat of our hearts
Or shall we let the song play on?
Are you saying what's on your mind?
Good
Then lets ponder the thoughts of each
Are you fighting the feelings I prescribe to you?
Don't
If I touch you, will you say stop?
Silence!
When I say I love you, do you say it back?
When I speak of nothing, do you speak?
When we embrace and you feel the way I touch you, I ask again,
Shall we dance?

SHUT OUT

Strengthened by powerful anxiety
Dropped below archives
Standing, reading everyone
Disguised as mist, listening to bullshit
No one to exaggerate emotions towards me
again
Close the doors,
For no one will visit.

BUS RIDE

I took a ride on that big bus
with nothing but drunks and whores
I sit and stare at these depressed prey
Am I one of them or maybe
something new
I reach out of the bus
to touch the breeze
and step out of this deserted and lonely road
to find that,
I am something real.

TRAVELING ALONE

A man walks along
a narrow path
Talking politics and sin
Not knowing where he is going
With hands in his pockets,
a bag at his side and a hat to be worn
He turns to notice
that no one is there.

WASTING TIME

Sitting in a chair,
smoking a cigarette
Quietly listening to the sounds
of the insects eager to get out.

The screaming sounds reminds
us that we are being looked
upon by shadows in the corner
as we try to escape

For we all are trapped
without an obvious exit.

FATHER?

"would you play with me?"
asks the young boy
"no!",
An answer comes from a deep voice
Is this man before me flesh and blood?
I don't understand
This man looks like me
He is always here, but does not notice me
Is this man flesh and blood
or a stranger?

EXQUISITE IN NATURE

Lost in a world of only
one beauty
She is relaxed by sounds
of the night
She takes in the fresh air
which make her sweat
She brings upon pain
that is softened
by the touch
of strong,
but sensitive hands
She looks in the mirror
to see the reflection
of her beauty
Her body is transparent
and she notices all
the inner beauty.

BEYOND A TOUCH

I stand in the corner
at a distance
Staring inside you
Trying to feel what your thinking
The light enhances your beauty
in a silhouette
I reach out
but I am unnoticed
I dance inside
to your thoughts
and my dreams
Two, in which should be one.

HOW HIGH?

I was too high to sleep
I was too high to eat
I was too high to walk
I was too high to talk
I was too high to think
I was too high to relate
I was just too high.

LIFE SAYS...

Death continues, a baby is born
The growth of something new
This has brought about a new poet
A poet of drugs, alcohol and satiable journeys.

Take a trip into the back of your mind
Pain is on one side, and the other,
open for you to claim
In that space feel free to conduct
any ceremony you wish

Move aside the pain
and retrieve your former life
renew your present
and enhance your living

this is a generation of minds to go on the
journey beyond
relax,
examine the roots and listen to the call of the wolves
don't be afraid
those are just traffic lights
go through
this is the entrance
to inner freedom.

MISSING YOU

A beautiful day
The smell of last night's perfume
swarms around me
I ponder away in my thoughts
as I lay alone
in this cool room,
A breeze blows through my soul
to create a better trip in my mind
My life is turning,
as if pages in a never ending book
Time to live
You & I, together
Shall embrace reality.

VOYAGE...

I'll take you to mystical
unknown places where there are nothing
but bright fires and light, which enhance
your mysterious and exotic look
Here, you'll speak not
While we stare in the curiousness
At the dancing of the serpents
On the while we'll expand
into each other's mind
to open the closed
Yours is written in hieroglyphics
That is what makes your beauty so
I'll touch your smooth, warm skin
which excites you
But this feeling is kept inside
For you are scared and happy
at the same time
Don't be afraid
I'm not here to hurt, but to learn

We'll make love in conversation
if that will soothe you
Don't wander off without finding
out what others don't know
Life is an erotic chance
For there is more inside
and beyond.

CROWDED THOUGHTS

This evil must escape my mind
It is dragging me down
Not letting me live
Leave, leave at once
I have to search for peace

CURIOUS AND COURAGEOUS

The elves wake before dawn
They creep out of the wilderness
searching for something new
Accepting whatever obstacles & evil
that would confront them
There are no lights or signs
The outcomes are unpredictable.

DESTROYING MINDS..

Look deep inside me, for I am human
and only human
Accept me, the things I say & do
there is only one me
that is so unique and original
with my own faults

I am caught up in something wonderful
and dangerous
I am learning to deal with this
Time and patience must be on my side
My blood runs thin
and my soul is weak
You have changed my human.

My heart pounds like a savage storm
as it waits for the touch of a sweet voice
I hold out my hand,
Will you grab it?

Don't let me fall without a kiss.

It's getting cold in here now
but it's not winter
The icicles descend from my heart
slowing me down

I look across the sea
that seems calm on top,
but confused inside
The confusion is masked
by beauty and mystery
Will she appreciate me and
accept my love that is eternal?

I am only human, unique
& original.
Know that I am something special
I can only give so much
Meet me halfway.

STARTING WITHOUT FEAR..

Enter into a world of happiness
A place never experienced before
Expand through this
and don't be afraid of your reactions
This is a place of rebirth
Where new life flows inside
It's an intense high
that you never want to come down from
Acknowledge the emotions
that surround you
Don't argue with them
Take that step in
Feel free to roam around
For this place is yours.

REACHING OUT

Looking into the dead air
grasping hold of something
that might not be there
Wanting this feeling to be shared
for sitting in the dark
I'm getting scared.

SPECIAL GIFT

All I ask is for one smile
Take hold of what I give
This is not to be taken advantage of
Death will soon be at your door
Are you frightened?
It's a trip to never, never land

FOOL'S PARADISE

Described as a castle builder
Idealist, visionary
or lustful thinker

I had a whimsical vision of bliss
You were there
We journeyed through the virgin forest
with complete serenity
The tranquility of the milieu
adorned your beauty
as angels eyed your presence with delight

I had a whimsical vision of bliss
You were there

DESI RE CANDIS

Smile with pride beautiful brown girl
It's the color they will see
The soul they will meet

If torn between color and society
The answer is apparent
Do not merge with society
Let the commonwealth adapt
to you

Smile with pride beautiful brown girl
It's the color they will see
The soul they will meet

Stick close to the roots of your skin
Clear the mind and lay tracks
to your heart

The merry dancers from the spirit
shine bright upon you
Allow your color to glisten above the earth
Never let your shade vanish
Your tint of Aphrodite is a passage
to peace

Smile with pride beautiful brown girl
It's the color they will see
The soul they will meet
They do not know the Beautiful Brown

(your color is a vision of independence and
your substance that expresses salvation)

LIFE SENTENCE

We have been found guilty
of relishing in the pond of self pity
We were sentenced to perish
in the destruction of our minds
We are eligible for parole
when peace inhabits the soul.

ENCOUNTER

Excuse me..
Come visit,
Or shall I assume
nature has visited your domain with gifts
Angels have sung on your paths
Is it ok to speak?
Ecstasy is my name

SPOKEN DESIRE

A tropic arrangement of flowers
Spring filled with beauty
to coincide with your
Vivacious individuality
Recognized,
Adored,
Playful,
Sagacious,
Angel of the mind,
Qualities of elegance.

A NEW YORK KNIGHT

Spare change? Spare change?
An empty cup filled with hope
A man burrowed in a soiled comforter,
with only his face displayed
People passing in their trendy fashions
Delivering a nod of disgust
Not a second to give greetings

Not known personally,
only stereotyped as a swimmer in a bottle

He may wet his lips on a bottle
but is there a difference between those who are
"fashionable" and this Knight?

Only the rank,
They are not degraded for a liquid diet
but applauded for the social company

Spare change?
Spare change?

DISBELIEVER

I'm recovering from being stoned
Prosecuted as love's idiot
by those who do not understand.

MOVING ON

It's raining in my life
Life only hurts once
Prepare to conquer fears
and set forth to new experiences
Excuse me while I rehearse the next routine
I'm out of practice.

DECEPTION

Have you seen the light?
The one illustrated?
Yes indeed you were deceived,
Your mind is laid to rest in the crypt
Sorrow swarms the genitalia of the soul
Awaken, you are brought to
Elysium.

IN CIRCLES

Walk into the obscure
with the blinds drawn
Rounding corners, going in circles
Ending up where I began
Seducing all the beauty nature has to offer
while reality stares at me with disgust

Reality is an exhibitionist..

APPLETON

Once I had a woman
Oh what a woman
So succulent, possessing all the beauty
that reigned around her,
her expressions and movements
hypnotize me as I gaze upon.

Once I had a woman,
so misunderstood
Wept inside at every sight,
only left with the
thoughts and memories (of her)
How they still remain so clear

I rehearse the moments spent many times over,
hoping that we would meet up again

Once I had a woman
To touch her flesh and linger
in her fragrance would purify
my cold and forgotten soul

Once I had a woman
Where is she now?

TRUE ARTISTRY

A utopian's vision,
with beauty in its simplicity
The incandescent eyes
to compliment the sable hair
which fades into the purity
of her flesh
A genuine ensemble
She floats above darkness
creating a warmth to all who surround.

To be held
To be touched
To create

I gain strength from her essence

"Mirable Visu"
(wonderful to behold)

EVERYDAY LIFE

Days are fading faster
Nights are getting longer
Burning fires, people's immoral desires
Crappin out on the role of the wind
The souls are sin...

THERESA MUCHA

9 months to birth
death instantaneously, unknowingly
A proclamation of faith and loyalty
angels have sung
With life no longer on this present earth
She is the smell of changing seasons
the voice of thunder
the flesh of rain
the breath of our air
the shining sun
She was called to journey a new passage

now reigns in "Empyrean"
(the highest Heaven)

FIERCE...

Pointing at the sky
What are you pointing at?
Sky of death
Death of loneliness and pity
That's where I want to be
At the end of the point
"High" where nothing can reach
or hurt
I'll find you there,
Waiting for the epitome of happiness.

FALSE HOPE

He dreamt of blue skies and warm shores
He dreamt of a woman with beauty,
Passion,
Independence,
Sensuality,
Intelligence,
Sense of humor

He dreamt of peace,
Of "love'

He dreamt
He never awoke.

UNTITLED

Creep towards the unknown
That's what we do
We sneak up to a situation we do not
want to understand.
When we get knowledge of what this is,
We head back and creep
to the next unknown.

The unknown or untouched
Is engulfed with more beauty inside
and out.
Once known or touched, the beauty fades away
Unless that individual keeps their ecstasies
and desires to the purest

A CHILD'S WORDS

"He's just a little prick!"
that's just my aunt,
she's drunk
the smell of liquor fills the air
along with the blinding fog
"I would rather argue with myself then come
to uncertain terms with my lethargic mother."
I'm leaving now. Do not follow me
I will roll dice to earn my life.

DO YOU REMEMBER...

The night we met?
Do you remember the night
We talked?
Danced?
Touched?
The alarm is sounding off
Awake from the other dimension
Thanks for the
Instrumental memories.

LIQUID BOTTLE

Reality is blurred when looked
at through an empty bottle
Insanity fills the innate soul
when the bottle is empty
Which road will lead me?

GRASPING FOR LIFE

A child sobs in a broken crib that
sits in the corner near an open window
The mother losing her patience,
drinking softly from a bottle that soaks up her thoughts
No one nearby to watch and keep safe
The wind is blowing the empty cupboards back and forth. The
fragrance of freshly sprayed glade
covers up the deathly aroma
Cigarettes burning one after another in an ash filled bin
Sirens from the outside are the only source of music

The three-room apartment,
cluttered with emptiness
The kettle whistling
blending in with the cry

No incentive..

SHELTERED BEAUTY

Standing in the cold with your only possession,
Your beauty
I approached from out of the darkness
and offered my services
You shuddered as I spoke,
as if I were a drifter

As I held the door to the shelter you were silent
A simple way to disguise your embarrassment

An introduction was not formerly conducted,
Only through thoughts

Agony was in my hands as I went to touch
and you were gone

Who left this young beauty to impersonate misery?

LETTER TO MICHELLE

A night such as this followed with an exchange
of gestures
Smiles were formed in the likeness of the light
The first encounter, hoping it not be the last
Hypnotizing me with natural beauty,
causing unsteadiness on my feet.

My mind wandering with the thoughts of caressing
the fair skin, to feel your body pressed against mine,
to touch those lips and hear you speak
We will stroll through the sacred fields
where the desire is pure

Accept my invitation to a journey
where ecstasy is the theme
Till the next encounter and new experience.

John

LIBBY

The innate beauty
complimenting the physical
I spontaneously drown in the passion
and sensitivity, leaving my soul in her care

Her movement so delicate and graceful
She is of brilliant art form
to be viewed with admiration

Fantasy and reality are one.

PURE

The angels play sweet music
while you dance
You expect nothing
The eyes are bright as aurora
The spring is near
Flowers bloom
representing change
You now dance in a different direction
to modify your soul

A seraph preserves your beauty
to be adored by all.

ORDINARY

Awakened from a somber sleep
I'm scorched by reality
Another dream took over
and created ominous outlooks
City lights pierced through my window
blinding me
The angel protected by fantasy,
I do not belong
She left without a warning
Closed
I'm an ordinary man.

SLEEPLESS WITHOUT

Since our last goodbye
The voice I heard
The shadow cast upon my wall
from the candle
The breeze blew away your image
let me sleep tonight

EPIGRAM

Is it the idea of her?
Or do I enjoy being with her?

Beauty
is only a disguise for hurt

THEATRE.. ACT I

There is enough bullshit in this world
Why create more?
Plenty of unfinished business, never ending games
played between the sexes
There are no true words ever spoken
Unless of course, there is something to gain

Creatures of greed, regroup,
peep at those victims who are
tormented and ridiculed by the
truculent ones

How much more before this Utopia
turns insane?

KYPRIS

So delicate in her smile
Pristine beauty unleashed to entice
the many a pawn that play
silhouettes to her flawless
cavity of solace

Hesitantly I release my fear
to enter into the marrow of her soul
I am a guest for a brief period of time,
for my existence within such a tranquil
place causes a stimulus of emotions
not yet experienced

So pleasing in her smile
Pure beauty is unleashed to tempt
the many a pawn that stare,
With eyes wide open upon her unblemished
Essence.

MELISSA

What next?
Pondering the thought of you
Ticking clock
I must go and meet with fate,
destiny
An messenger has visited without warning
what a delight
roses, daisies bloom new life
rebirth, conquer evil
The warm sweat of two combine
with one flesh
The breath of summer bliss
Feel the emotion touching the inner
The body dies
Soul and beauty do not.

PLAYING WITH DEATH

A bloodstained organ
Experiencing death
over and over
Russian roulette
Gods are in your favor
Ophidians thrive on the sin.

BAR SCENE

An illuminated smoke filled room
with fabricated conversation
as the liquor begins to supervise the night
Words, tarnishing the image of mortality
Bodies vibrating from one to the next
agitating potential prey
Flawless outlines are falsified to
conjure up a bedfellow

An illuminated smoke filled room

FINDING PEACE

How can I live without your
Touch?
Smell?
Kiss?
Exchange love, lovers we are
Intimate encounters, some pain
Some don't understand
Some don't want to understand
I was an explorer
Now I'm a hero
I found what people seek
Feelings exist
Fear divides the mind and heart
It is one

SWEET DEPARTURE

Brought you flowers
Wrote you poetry
Drank wine by candlelight
Got a smile

Flowers no longer live
The pen doesn't write
The candle has blown out
The smile has faded

"it's not you , it's me"

UNKNOWN PRESENCE

Longing for the love and touch
of a beauty so far away
Untouchable
Unattainable
Within reach
She can be seen through every thing that
defines happiness
Two worlds
Can she see me?
Can she feel me?
To know what excites her
To see her sleep
breathe, smile
My inspiration
will remain in the depths
Admiring her
Not forgetting her
Learning from her
Inhaling her

BORN AGAIN

The pedestal has gotten smaller
and my strength has weakened
The facade has been lifted
and all that was solid has
become transparent
You vanish to a place
where there is a higher plateau
of simplistic energy,
everyone there understands the life
as a freelancer, where there is beginning
and never an end, where opportunities
are abreast

I have reached that higher plateau
A zealous state, where the passion
flows and is secreted
Heterotopia has immersed

You have said goodbye, no ideals
Never to return

VOW TO LOVE

Love is not immediate beauty or physical attraction.
Love is made through communication, trust
and sincerity.

Love is devotion
from the Heart,
Mind
&
Soul
[Unconditional devotion].

Interminable love is
fulfilled through
absolute friendship.

If you seek love,
look within
yourself.

ADVICE

Enjoy the time that you have with her
Instead of thinking about the time
that you don't

WAITING

Comfortable in silence
Articulate in conversation
She stares with zeal
He is breathless for each encounter
Together, they define love

TRANSPARENCY

Soliloquies in motion
Thoughts rendered freely from the mouth
Omit the passion and substitute for anger
Swaying diligently on the emotions
of those captured by love
Love's fool, so arrogantly smitten by
the evil troth

Alas, wandering on the road of deceit,
searching on this incorrigible path
for divinity

Deception has been clear through its
queer and demeaning manner

REFLECTION

I just got high to escape the misery
that I am feeling
It's just a dream, a fantasy
Life is passing by while my eyes are closed
I am overlooking what's good and living my life
in the future, when there isn't one
if I continue this way
I need to wake up and see myself in the mirror
Get a good look at what I have become

RELIEF

Look out the window
and into the sky
That is where I will be

ABOUT THE AUTHOR

Growing up in Cambridge, MA has allowed the author to have the opportunity to experience a vast array of culture, and revisit that for every future endeavor. Although not all experiences were positive, they have paved a way to open up a mind that was once isolated. Moving forward, while trying to overcome fears and turmoil has been a struggle, but a struggle that has not beaten him. There is a connection with what is written and those paths he has crossed along the way. He tells a story in each word, phrase, poem that is written, with hope, that others will be able to relate and share to their own experiences, no matter who the reader is.

Made in United States
North Haven, CT
28 January 2024

48022975R00071